The Poetry of Dora Sigerson Shorter

Volume I – Verses

Dora Mary Sigerson was born in Dublin on August 16th, 1866, the daughter of George Sigerson, a surgeon and writer, and Hester (née Varian) also a writer.

Her father was a leader in Dublin's intellectual world and immersed the young Dora in the vibrant literary society of Dublin throughout her childhood, helping her gain a deep and complete love of her country. Like her father, Dora was active in the Irish literary revival, and a passionate campaigner for home rule.

Her poetry collections date from 1893 and are particularly evocative when she writes of her homeland, War and, most of all, the Easter Rising of 1916. Her friends included Katharine Tynan, the noted Irish poet and author as well as fellow writers and poets Rose Kavanagh and Alice Furlong

When she married Clement King Shorter, an English journalist and literary critic, in 1895 they moved to England and she wrote under the name Dora Sigerson Shorter. Although in England her heart's passion remained with Ireland.

The tragic events of Easter 1916, were a terrible blow to her and her health quickly began to fail.

Dora Mary Sigerson Shorter died on January 6th, 1918. The cause of her death was not disclosed.

As well as a foremost poet Dora's talents extended to sculpture, journalism and novels.

Dora's best-known sculpture is the memorial in Glasnevin Cemetery to the executed leaders of the Easter Rebellion.

In her lifetime she was renowned for her personal beauty and her charm. That charm is reflected in her works which are full of eagerness, love, sympathy, and, of course, suffering.

Index of Contents

LAST EVE
CEAN DUV DEELISH
GOOD-BYE!
DORA SIGERSON SHORTER – A CONCISE BIBLIOGRAPHY

DORA SIGERSON - A TRIBUTE AND SOME MEMORIES by Katharine Tynan

To think of Dora Sigerson—and it is a poignant thought—takes one back to Dublin in the 'nineties, or the later 'eighties. I think it was on a summer Sunday in 1887 that Dr. Sigerson came to see me with his two daughters and Rose Kavanagh, whom I already knew. The Yeatses were there that Sunday for the big meal at a most unfashionable hour, which was a feature of those years for the young writers and artists of Dublin. My old home was in the country, just under the Dublin mountains, and, I think, a very delightful place.

Everyone, of course, knew Dr. Sigerson by repute. The house was full of the young that day, with just a sprinkling of the young of heart like Mr. Yeats and my father and Dr. Sigerson. I remember that my brother said to me, "Miss Sigerson is very beautiful." She was. Her face then had some curious suggestion of the Greek Hermes. She wore her dark hair short, and it was in heavy masses. She had a beautiful brow and eyebrows, very fine grey eyes, a short straight nose, a warm pale colour, and vivid red lips. A little later the Irish-American, Miss Louise Imogen Guiney, dedicated her "Roadside Harp" to the Sigerson sisters:

There in the Druid brake,
If the cuckoo be awake
Again, oh, take my rhyme,
And keep it long for the sake
Of a bygone primrose-time.
You of the star-bright head
That twilight thoughts sequester:
You to your native fountains led,
Like to a young Muse garlanded:
Dora, and Hester.

Dora was indeed "like to a young Muse garlanded." She was singularly beautiful, with some strange hint of storm in her young beauty. She was so full of artistic impulse and achievement of many kinds, and she arrived at so much of art without any apprenticeship that the word "genius" seems not inapplicable to her. Our friendship flowed straight on from that summer Sunday of 1887. Dr. Sigerson's house in Clare Street became my headquarters when I went into Dublin from my country home. Dora was always painting or writing or doing sculpture. I can remember her coming from somewhere downstairs to the drawing-room at No. 3, Clare Street, when I was announced, wearing a sort of sculptor's blouse. There is still in her old home, crowded with beautiful things, at least one head by her of a nymph or a dryad, strangely delicate and pensive.

I don't think she had read much poetry till John O'Leary, saying her poetry was too introspective, gave her Percy's "Reliques," whence the genesis of her fine ballad poetry. If she had any training as an art student for her painting and drawing and sculpture, it must have been very slight. The gifts came to her out of the air, so to speak; real gifts and nothing acquired.

For seven good years my life was inextricably interwoven with hers and Hester's. We had the same friends, the same merry-makings, the same tastes and aims. We were of the circle which revolved around the great old Fenian, John O'Leary, and his not less noble sister; we visited the American poets, Mr. and Mrs. Piatt, at Queenstown, where Mr. Piatt was American Consul; we spent many happy days at Mr. Richard Ashe King's delightful house at Waltham Terrace, Blackrock. We wrote for the same papers. Presently Dora Sigerson and I were together in politics, both Parnellites when the "split" came. Together we attended Mr. Parnell's meetings; we went to meet him when he returned to Dublin from the country; we lived through all the passionate loyalty of those days. Together we exulted; together we mourned; together we followed our chief to the grave, not thinking upon how she should one day lie near him.

Perhaps the best holiday we had together was a scamper through Donegal on some business about the industries for Lady Aberdeen. It was just before I was married. From the time we left Amiens Street Station till we returned it was all pure enjoyment. The people with their beautiful manners, the wonderful scenery, the hotels, the car-drivers, the priests, the little towns, the wild, lonely places, the great hospitality—all were a delight to her. She was full of the joie de vivre, despite the hint of tragedy in her beauty. She did madcap things. Like Martin Ross she could mimic animals perfectly. How we laughed when she crowed like a cock over a low wall beyond which was a poultry-yard, and the real Vizier, after one careful look around, marshalled all his ladies into an inner enclosure. I have somewhere a book of that tour with her delightfully humorous drawings. She was always pencil in hand. We did the whole of Donegal within a fortnight, and came back, blowzed but happy, I to my wedding, she to the Dublin she always loved. A year or two later she met Clement Shorter at our little house in Mount Avenue, Ealing.

One thing I must not omit to mention—her passionate love of animals. In the old, good days in Dublin she used to pick up waifs and strays of forlorn doghood and take them to the Dogs' Home. The boys in the street used to shout derision at us: "Go on! wid yer grand hats and ye to be starvin' yer dog!" The sense of humour supported us.

How we laughed and lived together! Ah, well:

Let nothing disturb thee,
Let nothing affright thee.
All passes,
Only God remaineth
For ever and ever.

I will not speak of her beautiful poetry, essential poetry, always with a passionate emotion to give it wings. It is for the critic. No one will say she was not happy in her English life, though her heart was always slipping away like a grey bird to Ireland. She had a very full life and she had absolute devotion and knew what a precious thing she had.

Her breakdown in health was sudden. She attributed it herself to her intense and isolated suffering—isolated beyond the perfect sympathy of her devoted husband—over the events following Easter week, 1916, in Dublin, and the troubles which menaced the country she adored. I think she need not have felt so bitterly isolated; the spirit of humanity is strong in the good English—and the good English are very good—but the fact remains that she broke her heart over it all; and so she died, as she would have chosen to die, for love of the Dark Rosaleen.

DORA SIGERSON by C. P. Curran

The finest side of Irish life and literature is poorer to-day by the death of Dora Sigerson. From her long residence in England she was known here mainly as a poet of a genius as distinguished as it was personal. But when, in recent years, affairs in Ireland grew more critical, her great-hearted personality emerged more clearly and shone the more brightly as the situation grew more dangerous. Love of Ireland was with her a passion. The events of Easter week moved her profoundly. She spent herself regally on behalf of her people with brain, pen and fortune and at the expense of her vitality. The best of the English weeklies said that "the rebellion killed her almost as surely as if she had stood with the rebels in O'Connell Street. Henceforth she could think of little else; of what had died with it and what might live." That is no less than the truth. She is fairly to be reckoned with the dead of Easter. Devotion to their cause consumed her like a flame into which she flung all her gifts, neither few nor negligible. She was a true artist, eagerly seeking expression for an ardent and manifold personality which itself transcended all her work, whether in poetry, sculpture or painting. Her poetry was saluted by the greatest contemporary names in England: Meredith, Francis Thompson, Swinburne, and the present writer has seen her name as the subject of lecture on the noticeboards of the Sorbonne. What faults lay on the surface of her verse were more than compensated for by its intensity, an intensity often tragic, "stoned by continual wreckage of her dreams," but always filled with pity. In the "Songs of the Irish Rebellion" and in her later work generally which we, in Ireland, will always consider her best, the passion that consumed her burnt away these superficial defects, themselves characteristic of her impetuous spirit. The poet of "Ireland," of the "Wind on the Hills," of "Ceann Dubh Dilis," of "Sixteen Dead Men," will always be remembered on that honourable roll of artists who, to the gain of both, fused with their art, the strong love of the people.

THE PATH OF LIFE

IN the springtime once I wandered 'mid fair flowers of golden hue;
Wonder-eyed I gazed around me in those fields where all was new,
And a path stretched long before me, soft with moss and blossoms white,
While the birds, so sweetly singing, filled my soul with fresh delight.
Down the path, with song and laughter, came three maidens hand in hand.
By their side a shadow glided that I could not understand:
For I scarce could see it coming, yet I knew that it was there.
Like a cloud upon the brightness of a sky that was all fair—
Maids more beauteous than the blossoms of the flowers which deck the lea,

Maids more joyous than the happy birds that flit from tree to tree.
'Tell me who thou art,' I pleaded, 'thou with eyes of peace and love?'
'I am Hope,' she softly whispered, pointing with white hand above.
'Who art thou whose fair cheek flushes, 'neath the kiss of health, so red.

Thou with restless limbs and slender?'—'I am Youth,' she gladly said.
'Who art thou,' I questioned further, 'thou with glance of merriment?'
'We are sisters three,' she answered, 'Hope, Youth, Joy, from Heaven sent.'
Then the dim lips of the shadow moved—I heard a faint voice call:
'On! on! Time must never linger; Death, the king, is end of all.'

So along the path we wandered—oh! the bliss of those short hours!
Youth and Hope and Joy together 'mid the everblooming flowers
That on life's smooth path were glowing soft beneath my naked feet.
Till I envied nought in Heaven, thinking here my lot complete.

As I raised the flowering branches that across my path would stray,
Lo! I found amidst the blossoms at my feet Love sleeping lay.
'Wake!' I cried, 'my soul would know thee. Stranger, wake! my heart is thine.'
At my call he woke and, rising, laid his burning hand in mine.
'Thou art Love,' I said, 'and fairer than all things that God hath made;
Joy itself must have an ending, Youth is only born to fade,
And alone Love is immortal, faithful Love can never die—
Death's dark gates for him are open. Death himself must let him by.'
Then my heart grew chill, for nigh me once again I heard that call:
'On! on! Time can never linger; Death, the king, is end of all.'

So along the path we wandered, pausing oft for sweet caress.
Till my heart felt overflowing with its wealth of happiness;
But lo! on the path before us briars mingled with the moss,

And the flowers died on the branches, but I did not feel their loss.
What cared I, with Love beside me, if the sun should hide its light?
He was summer, *he* was sunshine, by his side there was no night.
Rougher grew the path before us, and the hedges lost their bloom.
Stretching out their thorny branches like long fingers in the gloom.
Then Love lingered slow behind me, saying, 'Dear, I cannot stay,
For my feet are weary toiling o'er this rough and thorny way,
For the flowerless branches wound me—for the sun has ceased to shine.
And I dread the growing darkness strange with shapes I can't define.'
So I watched them quick departing; Joy and Love went side by side.
'O my Love, why hast thou left me?' in my grief I sadly cried;
'Love braves all and fears no evil, Love gives all unselfishly.
There's no darkness, there's no danger, there's but Love where Love can be.

Love makes smooth the roughest pathway, Love makes bloom the budless bough—
Youth and Hope thou takest with thee: must I lonely wander now?
And the way so steep before me, wanting thee I could not climb;
No! I'll trace our happy footprints backwards o'er the path of Time.'
But alas I how vain my hoping— on my ears those dread words fall:
'On! on! Time knows no returning; Death is king and end of all.'

Lone I journeyed on, and Sorrow rose with pale cheeks by my side,

Weeping oft that Love had left me, sighing oft that Youth had died;
And a dread shape strode before me, with wild eyes and streaming hair,
Then my heart grew cold with anguish, for I knew this was Despair.
But some hand from out the darkness drew her back into the night,
And the sky grew fair, for Heaven shed upon my path its light.
'Hope!' I cried, 'thou hast returned; bring'st thou back my Love to me?'

'No!' she said, 'thy Love was worthless, he has gone and set thee free.
On Life's path two flowers are blooming, one grows gaudy, bright, and tall.
But the other fair and lowly—oft a heedless foot will fall
Crushing down each snowy petal that had sprung from Heaven's seed:
Thou hast passed the purer blossom by to pluck the flaunting weed
Thou hast sought for sun and sunshine, where to seek thou didst not know,
For thou'st caught the vague reflection here upon the earth below.
If the true sun thou art seeking, thou must turn thine eyes above—
Thou hast feared Death as he followed—he would give thee Life and Love.
Mourn not Love that proved so worthless, there's a purer Love on high—
Mourn not Joy, for Joy is living, yea, a Joy that cannot die.
Mourn not Youth, for Death would lead thee on where years can never be—
As a grain of sand thy life is on that shore—Eternity.

On! and weary not in going, let thy heart obey that call;
On! for Earth holds nought to mourn for—on! for Death gives life to all.'

MAN'S DISCONTENT

WHITE feet half hid in violets, small hands in a burden fair,
A burden of Spring's first blossoms she wove for her neck and hair
Into wreaths, as she paused a moment on the threshold of maidenhood.
O my child love! hesitating, there I met her as she stood.
So I stayed till I grew weary—man's discontent, I ween—
Then I thought I longed for Summer, with trees for ever green.
1 tired of primrose blossoms and the budding boughs of spring,
And the chirp! chirp! of this year's birds that had not learned to sing.
I thought her soft arms too slender, and the smooth young cheek too clear,

And the April eyes that loved me too ready with smile or tear,
Too ready to read my wishes in mine that she might obey
Ere I spoke; so in the springtime I went from her arms away.

I sought my love and I found her, when Summer days were long,
All the hedges bright with blossoms and musical with song,
But the eyes that saw me coming no answer to mine would speak;
The lids drooped till the lashes lay dark on her crimson cheek,
The hands I clasped for a moment would but struggle to be free,
As I tried to win her to speak of love, of herself, of me.

'Hark! the young birds,' she only said; 'dost hear them sing in the wood?'
Love's rosy wings had brushed her eyes as she passed to maidenhood.
So I stayed, but soon grew weary — man's discontent, I ween —
And I longed for Autumn colours, not trees for ever green.

Cried I: 'Its sky at sunset is far more fair than this.'
Then I thought, my love's cheek flushes too ready 'neath my kiss,
That the gentle voice replying spoke love too timidly.
And the shy hands culling blossoms had no caress for me.
I tired of roses' perfume and the song the wild-birds sung,
So I left her in the noon-time, when Summer yet was young.

'Neath the sunset skies of Autumn, all the heath-clad hills flushed red;
Sweet the lark his matins singing in the blue sky over-head.
And the languid breeze was perfumed by a rose's stolen breath;
'Twas the last white bud of Summer that escaped the hand of death,
And my sweet, I feared to meet her for my yesterday of scorn;
Then I flung myself beside her as she knelt amid the corn.
She only said: 'To red and gold grew the green young leaf of Spring.
The rose filled the dead cowslip's throne; now poppy reigns a king.'

Then she sighed, with blue eyes tearful and quivering lips that smiled,
'And to womanhood's perfection came the promise of the child.
But the rose and cowslip withered, and the poppy's death is nigh.
For the changing leaf that lingers there remains nought but to die.
Through the bitter winds of Winter let me shelter by thy side;
Prithee, stray not with the Autumn, O my love ! unsatisfied.'

So I stayed, but soon grew weary — man's discontent, I ween —
Of the woods all clad in splendour, rarest red, and gold, and green;
Of the hands that toiling for me pressed the red juice from the vine.
And brought the fragrant peaches that I might not trouble mine;
Of the fawn-like eyes that watched me, ever speaking of their love;
Of the neck I once thought softer than the white breast of a dove.
So I rose up from my resting ere the Autumn days were dead,

And the oak, and beech, and chestnut had not yet their bright leaves shed;
While the birds were singing gaily from their shelter in the thorn,
Still the sleep-bestowing poppies lit their red lamps in the corn.

I sought my love in the Winter, for I sorrowed for the past,
And in the long nights of thinking I knew my own heart at last;
That mine were the imperfections that I seemed in her to find.
That happiness ever beside me made me to sorrow grow blind.
How I of God's gifts grew weary — man's discontent, I ween —
That to-day sighs for to-morrow, then to weep for what had been.
She was sleeping when I found her, O my love! in one hand lay
Spring's young buds and Summer roses with their fair bloom passed away;

But the poison-breathing poppy on her lip was lying red.
Ah! the sleep-bestowing poppy had left me but the dead;

The calm eyes gazing heavenwards could not see the love mine bore,
And the pale brow 'neath my kisses still its marble colour wore;
Till the snow that was not whiter hid the silent face from me —
Hid the lips that could not answer and the eyes that could not see.
Flake by flake came down and hid her from the cold sky overhead
Thus, having all, I lost all, ere the Winter days had fled.

SPRING SONG—TO IRELAND

Weep no more, heart of my heart, no more!
The night has passed and the dawn is here,
The cuckoo calls from the budding trees,
And tells us that Spring is near.

Sorrow no more, beloved, no more;
For see, sweet emblem of hope untold!
The tears that soft on the shamrocks fall
There turn to blossoms of gold.

Winter has gone with his blighting breath,
No more to chill thee with cold or fear.
The brook laughs loud in its liberty,
Green buds on the hedge appear.

Weep no more, life of my heart, no more!
The birds are carolling sweet and clear;
The warmth of Summer is in the breeze.
And the Spring—the Spring is here.

DAISIES

Blossomed too soon, little daisies of Spring!
Leaving the sheltering arms of the earth,
The white tears of Winter unshed in the sky.
And weary-eyed Sorrow to welcome your birth.

See, 'twas cold Winter that woke you from sleep.
Breathed upon you with Summer's warm breath,
Kissed your eyes open with lips of the Spring,
Waked you too early—to winter and death.

Where is the promise he whispered to you—
The warmth of the sunshine, the cool of the breeze.
The perfume of thorns all heavy with bloom.
The linnet's sweet song from his shade in the trees?

Bird-songs are silent, and branches are bare;
The snow makes a crown on the heights of the hill;
And your stricken blossoms lie crushed on the ground.
For the warm breath that wooed you to life groweth chill.

Cover, white snowflakes, the spot where they lie,
Scarce living the length of a winter's short noon.
Oh! cover them whitely that no one may find
The grave of my daisies that blossomed too soon.

THE OLD VIOLON

'Going, going!' the voice was loud,
And, rising, silenced the chattering crowd.
'Going! going! shall it be gone?'
The auctioneer held up an old violon.
'The mute though tarnished is silver still,
The aged strings have not lost their skill.'
They laughed in scorn as he praised the case.
The ebon nuts and the polished face—
Jokingly betted together that none
Could draw a tune from the old violon.
When lo ! from out of their midst appeared
A man of countenance strange and weird,
With gentle touch laid his thin hand on
The polished face of the old violon.
'Thou scorned, thou worthless,' the stranger said
'Wake, heart of music, art thou too dead?'
As though some spirit long slept awoke,
A faint, low sigh from his fingers broke.

He took the bow in his trembling hand,
So old was he that he scarce could stand,
And still as death grew the auction hall.
For fear and silence fell over all.
They knew, as they watched in awed surprise.
He read their hearts with his piercing eyes,
And graven there in the long ago
Each story that sprang from beneath his bow.
He sang of love, and then years of pain

Rolled back—they dreamt they were young again;
The wife looked up to her husband's face.
And once more saw there the manly grace
That won her love when her heart was young
(Ah! 'twas the past that the violon sung);
And he, looking back, saw that once more
The faded cheek was as fresh as of yore;
Out from his eyes beamed the old love light,
And taking her hand, he pressed it tight.
The violon rang through the hall once more—
A mother cried for the babe she bore.
And stretching her empty arms out wide,
She felt no longer her wish denied;
The downy head lay upon her breast.
The tiny hands her pale cheek caressed.
To her lonely heart joy and comfort fell
From those wordless lips that can plead so well.

The violon's song rang loud and clear:
They saw a garden all fair appear,
Perfumed with roses and blossoms white,
Lifting their heads to the sun's hot light.
A statue stood there amidst them all—
A cry of wonder went down the hall—
For at its base, kneeling all alone,
Pressing warm lips to the feet of stone,
Raising soft hands to the face above,
A maiden was breathing her soul in love.
Gold-hearted lilies and roses sweet
She culled and laid at the statue's feet,
But touching the stone each flower would die.
The maid arose with a mournful cry.
And glanced in fear round the garden fair:
It was weeds and thorns that flourished there.
'O love,' she cried, 'I am sore afraid—
The night has come and my blossoms fade.'
Raising her arms to the stony face,
The statue fell at her slight embrace;
Down at her feet her idol lay—
An empty shell was this broken day.
Amidst the fragments she sought to find
Her god of Beauty, her love so kind.
Her faith, her hopes, that were scattered all;
Her cry was echoed within the hall;

Therein one young face so pale it grew,
That those who saw it her story knew.

Then of the present the violon sang.
No words it gave them yet as it rang;
Each heart gave words to the wondrous lay:
'The living present is ours to-day.'
And now they shudder and hold their breath,
The violon's song is the song of death—
Death in most cruel and dreadful guise—
The god of war rose before their eyes.
The clash of arms filled the auction hall,
Blood seemed around and over all,
Each woman shrank to her husband's side,
He clenched his hand as he rose and cried.
The cry of battle, the eagle's cry,
That sights his quarry from far on high,
For his heart beat quick with the lust for blood;
He fain would seek in that ruddy flood
To quench that fierce, unsatiable thirst
With which man and beast are alike accurst.

And now a moment, so strange and still
They seemed enchained to the violon's will—
So silent all that an echo flew
From the sobbing breath that a strong man drew-

When sudden there broke a fearful cry
That seemed to quiver across the sky,
A cry of some soul, it was to those
Who heard it, a soul in life's last throes,
A cold, passing breath from death's black wings,
A crash of discord o'er broken strings;
And what had been was now no more,
Silence and death seemed to cloud them o'er;
The past, the present, all men may see.
But no man knoweth what is to be.
Again they start with a new surprise.
No minstrel is there to their wildered eyes,
From whence he came or whither he fled.
Or of the living, or of the dead.
Their wondering hearts have never known.
The violon lay on the desk alone.
Fearing to lose, yet afraid to win.
Their voices rise, and above their din—
'Going! going! 'tis gone! 'tis gone;
A rare Stradivarius this old violon.
Behold!' and the auctioneer thought to raise
It high in his hand as he sung its praise—
With a faint, low sob, like a passing bell,
To dust 'neath his hand the violon fell.

INNOCENCE

White rose must die all in the youth and beauty of the year,
Though nightingale should sing the whole night through,
Though summer breezes woo,
She will not hear.

Too delicate for the sun's kiss so hot and passionate.
Or for the rude caresses of the wind,
She dropped and pined —
They mourned too late.

Birds carol clear :
'Summer has come,' they say,
'O joy of living on a summer's day!'
White rose must die all in the youth and beauty of the year.

KING AND FATHER

Mountains and vales, how ye quake 'neath His tread—
Wake from your slumbers, He calls, O ye dead!
Tremble, great trees, bowing down 'neath His breath;
Lay by thy scythe, at His bidding. King Death!
The sun in the heavens grows pale at His wrath.
And the stars, at a glance, disappear from their path.
God, at Thy feet, then, awe-stricken we fall—
Lord of the universe, Maker of all!

Earth's secret treasures lie bare to Thy sight,
Nor hidden from Thee the dark deeds of the night;
The lion grows timid, fawns low at Thy feet;
The waves from the shore at Thy bidding retreat.
Thou speakest—the monarch's proud ruling is o'er;
His power and his riches avail him no more,
Endless Thy greatness—of Thee are all things;
Endless Thy glory, O King of all Kings!

When mountains belched forth their red flames to the sky,
And Heaven's forked tongues thundered back in reply;
When the sun, in his horror, recoiled at the sight,
And earth hid her brow in the darkness of night;
When stars into dust fell, and vanished in space,
And but man, in his blindness, laughed up in Thy face—

Endless Thy mercy. Thy strong hand was still—
O Crucified Lord upon Calvary's hill!

Yet, Thou forgettest all. Father above,
Remembering nought but Thine infinite love:
Stretching those wounded Hands out to our aid;
Telling us tenderly, "Be not afraid !"
Ready to help us, if only we call—
Nothing too weak for Thee, nothing too small;
Ready to hear, when we kneel on the sod;
Thou our Redeemer, our Father, our God!

THE HIGHWAY TO FAME

In every man this world doth hold
Two selves are cast in that human mould.
If he hearken but to the voice of one,
Then heaven is his when his work is done ;
But if to the other his ear doth turn,
Despair in his heart shall for ever burn.

I and my other self one day
Woke from sleep on the world's highway.
Women and men bore us company,
But never a child did I chance to see.
I pitied young faces so pale and wan
I saw in the crowd, as we hurried on.
I pitied old faces, so eager they
Lest they be last on the great highway.
Another road we have met at last —
We paused a moment ere it we passed.
Few turned their feet the strange road upon.
Though the way was fair God's sun shone on.

The path was rough, but the hedges' bloom
Sent forth a sweet and a rare perfume.
If the thorns wounded your naked feet,
The birds' songs were in your ear full sweet.
Did you close your eyes in black despair,
You oped on the hills—and God was there.
Did you weep with fear when the night came on,
The face of Hope in the darkness shone.
'O stay,' I cried, 'for a moment stay—
Till I pluck from the hedge a wild-rose spray.
Hark, the sweet birds! For a moment stay—
No song I hear on the world's highway,

But cries of women and men alway.'

My other self thus replied to me:
'Then the hill of Fame you will never see,
Nor hear the songs so wondrous there'—
And I passed the road that I deemed so fair.
Suspicion, envy, and jealousy,
I oft in my neighbours' eyes could see.
Alas! in my heart the serpent grew—
I smiled lest others should see it too.
A woman staggered, and falling cried
As I paused a moment by her side:
'Too late, too late! I am lost for aye,
I have passed God's road on the great highway
I have missed the treasure that lies before,

And glimpse of Heaven Til see no more.'
I laid my hand her cold brow upon,
But my other self in my ear said: 'On!
For those behind will help her through.'
I stepped in her place, but that cry I knew
Was the last she gave, ere she silent lay
'Neath the cruel feet on the great highway.

A cottage door, as we passed, stood wide;
A mother sat with her babe inside,
And her eyes beamed love as she kissed the child,
That raised its arms in its sleep and smiled:
In the fields that bordered the great highway
Children dropped, as we passed, their play.
I raised a bright guinea for them to see—
A golden king-cup they held to me.
A sapphire's gleam from my finger fell—
They gathered a bunch of the blue speedwell.
A string of pearls I raised again—
Laughing, they turned to their daisy chain.
A youth and a maiden I next did see;
I cried in my heart, 'He will envy me.'
He smiled as he kissed the white hand that lay
In his, and I sighed on the great highway.
Is it worth all I lose and I leave behind,
That treasure I seek, which I may not find?

I saw a man in my path, and he
Stood still as we came, and he looked at me.
Oh, sorrow's home was that face divine;
Oh, the infinite love as his eyes met mine!
An oaken cross on his shoulders lay—

I paused a moment, then turned away.
For my other self thus had cried to me:
"Tis but a phantom you chance to see.
Look! Even now it has ceased to stay
'Neath the hurrying feet on the great highway.'

So I was first in the weary race,
As, aged and worn, we toiled apace.
Each man bowed low at my feet and came
To crown me king on the Hill of Fame,
And king of them all I reigned alone.
Yet I shuddered oft on my golden throne.
The ground had grown not earth nor stones,
For the hill was raised of dead men's bones.
I fear my subject's untiring praise,
For his hand the while with his dagger plays.
My other self whispers: 'O joy! for see,
Men and women all worship thee.
Thy flattered ear to their praise incline;
Endless glory and wealth are thine;
Such fame, such worship, no man hath known.'

Ah me! I sigh on my golden throne.

LITTLE WHITE ROSE

Little white rose that I loved, I loved,
Roisin ban, Roisin ban!
Fair my bud as the morning's dawn.
I kissed my beautiful flower to bloom,
My heart grew glad for its rich perfume—
Little white rose that I loved.

Little white rose that I loved grew red,
Roisin ruad, Roisin ruad!
Passionate tears I wept for you.
Love is more sweet than the world's fame—
I dream you back in my heart the same,
Little white rose that I loved!

Little white rose that I loved grew black,
Roisin dub, Roisin dub!
So I knew not the heart of you.
Lost in the world's alluring fire,
I cry in the night for my heart's desire,
Little white rose that I loved!

TIME AND THE LADY

Haste, maiden, haste! the spray has come to budding,
The dawn creeps o'er the heavens gold and fair.
Come, see the bud ere breaking, the languid day awaking.
'A moment. Time, until I bind my hair.'

Come, maiden, come! the bud has burst to blossom,
The sun has kissed the earth and found it sweet.
Come, lest you lose, adorning, the beauty of the morning.
'A moment, Time, a moment, till I eat.'

Come, maiden, come! ripe fruits are on the branches,
The evening star is glowing in the blue;
The breeze's breath grows colder. Come ere the day is older!
'A moment till I sip—I'm then with you.'

Quick, maiden, quick! Death's hand has stripped the leafing;
Night frees her clouding hair from bonds that keep.
Quick! lest you're lost for ever, in the gloom to find me never.
'A moment. Time, a moment, till I sleep.'

A ROSE WILL FADE

You were always a dreamer, Rose, red Rose,
As you swung on your perfumed spray,
Swinging, and all the world was true,
Swaying, what did it trouble you?
A rose will fade in a day.

Why did you smile to his face, red Rose,
As he whistled across your way?
And all the world went mad for you.
All the world it knelt to woo.
A rose will bloom in a day.

I gather your petals, Rose, red Rose,
The petals he threw away.
And all the world derided you;
Ah ! the world, how well it knew
A rose will fade in a day.

WHO IS HE?

Who is he, dying so hard?
Hard is it to die—
Die in the warmth of June,
Bird and bee in tune—
Die in the singing time.
When all the world's in rhyme.
Hard it is to die.

He is Hope lying so low,
Dull it is to lie—
Lie, and the hounds full cry
Give music to each sigh—
Lie, and the antlered stag
Leaps light from crag to crag.
Weary 'tis to lie.

Is there never a one to weep?
Weep, for Hope is dead.
Dead, and a body so fair.
Never a woman to care?

Untuneful is laughter and mirth;
Hide him, then, under the earth.
Well it were to be dead.

Here comes one weeping so hard:
Woeful 'tis to weep.
Tears on the cheek of youth.
Where smiles should be in truth;
Tears in the eyes of love.
Angels should weep above,
When the young are sad below.
Better were death than woe;
Hard it is to weep.

ALL SOULS' NIGHT

[There is a superstition in some parts of Ireland that the dead are allowed to return to earth on the 2nd of November (All Souls' Night), and the peasantry leave food and fire for their comfort, and set a chair by the hearth for their resting before they themselves retire to bed.]

O Mother, mother, I swept the hearth, I set his chair and the white board spread,
I prayed for his coming to our kind Lady when Death's sad doors would let out the dead;

A strange wind rattled the window-pane, and down the lane a dog howled on.
I called his name and the candle flame burnt dim, pressed a hand the door-latch upon.
Deelish! Deelish! my woe forever that I could not sever coward flesh from fear.
I called his name and the pale Ghost came; but I was afraid to meet my dear.

O mother, mother, in tears I checked the sad hours past of the year that's o'er,
Till by God's grace I might see his face and hear the sound of his voice once more;
The chair I set from the cold and wet, he took when he came from unknown skies
Of the land of the dead, on my bent brown head I felt the reproach of his saddened eyes;
I closed my lids on my heart's desire, crouched by the fire, my voice was dumb.
At my clean-swept hearth he had no mirth, and at my table he broke no crumb.
Deelish! Deelish! my woe forever that I could not sever coward flesh from fear.
His chair put aside when the young cock cried, and I was afraid to meet my dear.

THE FAIRIES

The fairies, the fairies, the mischief-loving fairies.
Have stolen my loved one, my darling, and my dear;
With charms and enchantments they lured and waylaid him.
So my love cannot comfort and my presence cannot cheer.

The fairies, the fairies, I'll love no more the fairies;
I'll never sweep the hearth for them or care the fairy thorn,
I'll skim no more the yellow cream nor leave the perfumed honey;
But I'll drive the goats for pasture to their greenest rath each morn.

With Ave, and Ave, and many a Paternoster,
Within their magic circle I'll tell my beads for you;
My prayers be sharp as arrows to pierce their soulless bosoms
Till they come with loud sorrow to tell me that they rue.

My darling, my darling, what glamour is upon you
That you find for your gaze satisfaction and content
In the charms of that colleen, with her black snaky ringlets,
Her red lips contemptuous, and her gloomy brows so bent?

The fairies, the fairies, from her blue eyes were peeping;
They blew her hair about you, so you were lost, my dear.
With their charms and enchantments they lured and waylaid you,
So my love cannot comfort and my presence cannot cheer.

A FAIRY PRINCE

Prince Charming, when the wizard's wand
Had wrecked for aye my fairyland;
Had razed my castles to the earth,
And killed my child's heart with his mirth;
Then weeds grew rank where flowers had been,
And slow snakes flashed their length between.

Prince Charming, when the darkness came,
With many tears I called your name,
And 'Give me back my fairyland!'
You took me by the willing hand
Ere day had lit the dawn's pale flame;
You left me when the darkness came.

Prince Charming, spite of wizard's wand.
You said you'd find my fairyland.
I open eyes too sad for tears—
Nought but an open grave appears.

AT CHRISTMAS TIME

For that old love I once adored
I decked my halls and spread my board
At Christmas time.
With all the winter's flowers that grow
I wreathe my room, and mistletoe
Hangs in the gloom of my doorway,
Wherein my dear lost love might stray
When joy-bells chime.

What phantom was it entered there
And drunk his wine and took his chair
At Christmas time?
With holly boughs and mistletoe
He crowned his head, and at my woe
And tears I shed laughed long and loud;
'Cet back, O phantom! to thy shroud
When joy-bells chime.'

A CHANGELING

My Future lay cradled asleep;
I kissed the sweet mouth and she smiled
With a promise of all she should be,

Womanhood crowning the child—

Her wings that would grow with her growth,
Till they bore her to heaven at last;
When she queened in the world awhile,
Then all the sweet mockery past.

So closing my eyes while I dreamt.
Thus praying on her behalf,
I could but think I had slept.
For I woke with an elfin laugh.

What fairy had crept through the door
To leave me this changeling child.
Who looked on my tears with a laugh.
And mocked at my prayers as she smiled?

SORROW

Into my heart, Sorrow, you found a way;
Mine enemy, it was bitter to weep and pray;
I gave you tears for drinking,
And heart-sick sobs,
With brain too sick for thinking,
And to the throbs
Of my sad heart I hushed you till I crushed you
Into rest for all your thorns.

Into my heart. Sorrow, too oft you came;
Mine enemy, I heed not nor dread your name.
Frozen the stream of your quaffing.
And now your rest
Is broken with my laughing.
To my breast
In these mine arms I hush you till I crush you
Into rest for all your thorns.

THE LITTLE BROTHER

O Brother, brother, come down to the crags by the bay,
Come down to the caves where I play;
For, oh! I saw on the rocks, asleep,
A fair mermaid, and the slow waves creep
To bear her away, away.

O brother, brother, come quick till you laugh with me,
For no mermaid so fair is she,
But the little lass that I saw last night
(I hid in the shade, you stood in the light),
And she weeping so bitterly.

O brother, brother, I watched her through the day,
Saw her hair grow jewelled with spray ;
Once her cheek was brushed by a gull's wet wing.
And a finch flew down on her hand to sing.
And was not afraid to stay.

O brother, brother, will she soon awakened be?
I would that she laugh with me.
She sleeps, and the world so full of sound—
She's so deaf, like the dead that are under the ground,
That I laugh and laugh to see.

MY DARLING

My darling laughed in the dawning,
And the birds perched low to hear.
The quick sprung anew from dead ashes
That Spring's passing feet had flung clear.
Oh, Life came over the meadows,
And the song of her coming was sweet;
The streams leaped joy-mad down the mountains,
Flowers bloomed 'neath her dawning feet.
The trees bent their branches fruit-laden,
So low as her soft hands' hold;
And the harvest rose up like an army
Of kings in their harness of gold.
Oh, Life came over the meadows
From her home behind the sun;
No mind could guess whence her being.
Where she went when her work was done.
As she danced, danced Death the cold shadow
That was cast by her body so fair.

My darling laughed in the dawning,
Lifers hand on her sunny hair.

My darling slept in the dawning,
Then came to my heart a fear;
For peace may be lost in the darkness.

And joy be drowned in a tear.
I whispered : 'Sleep in the singing,
When the buds are breaking to bloom.
Each branch with its load low-swinging,
Each flower with its faint perfume;
When the world is young with laughter,
Mankind on his throne a king.
When the soul sings of a Hereafter,
And is not ashamed to sing.'
Then Life faded into her shadow.
And Death took her form and was fair.
My darling smiled in her sleeping,
Death's hand on her sunny hair.

LOVE IN MY ARMS LIES SLEEPING

Roses red for the fair young head to weave a crown,
Let them be half blown,
For a rose in June it will fade too soon to gold and brown.
For thee my own
The fairest blossoms in all love's land, for that small hot and,
And a bird to sing all the sweet day through,
Lest fear should wake in the heart of you,
And I hear my own heart's beating;
Wild roses red for the fair gold head.
Love in my arms lies sleeping.

Lilies fair for the wind-blown hair,
It were better so
Than a blossom dead.
And a rose's thorn; but the fresh glad morn brings breath of snow.
Hath summer fled?

Hath winter come when I dreamt it spring?
Is my sweet bird dead that he does not sing?
I hear but my heart's sad weeping.
Loose and cold is thy soft hands' hold;
Love in my arms lies sleeping.

WINTER IN SUMMER

All in a bleak December
My heart had summer time;
Crouched by the glowing ember,

We found an Eden's clime.
The storm that shook the casements
Made laughter in my ears;
No frown thy gloom, December,
Sweet rain that was not tears.

All in the month of roses
My heart is like to die;
Now winter's gloom encloses,
We thought it passed us by;
And so my young companions
Fall laughing back from me:
For dreary melancholy
Is no good company.

O who can smile in summer,
When winter rules their heart?—
When pleading lips grow dumb, or
Clasped hands fall apart?
White cheeks more chill than snowing,
Dull eyes so full of rain,
Pale lips that part for sighing.
Where is your summer's gain?

Or who'd weep in December,
Whose heart with summer glows?
O who would e'er remember
Bare branches, or the rose?
Smooth cheeks flush pink as blossoms.
Red lips and laughter rhyme;
O would June were December,
I wot 'twas summer time.

HOW LONG WILT THOU LOVE ME?

How long wilt thou love me, O my love?
'As long as life may be.'
Life is but a breath
Breathed us by Death,
That we may learn and be the makers of our Destiny.
How long wilt thou love me, O beloved?

'So long shall I love thee, O my love!
As long as time may be.'
Time's but the go and come
Of a clock's pendulum.

Made so we count and see a cycle of Eternity.
How long wilt thou love me, O beloved?

'So long shall I love thee, O my love!
As long as tears may be.'
Tears may turn to laughter
In the long Hereafter.
Laughter to tears for me, as is in our God's decree.
How long wilt thou love me, O beloved?

'So long shall I love thee, O my love!
As long as love may be,
Love that can courage give
To the faint heart to live.
To the faint heart Death to see, love that is Eternity,
So long shall I love thee, O my love!'

A WAYWARD ROSE

Mischevious rose from the rose-tree swaying,
Can I not bind thee nor hold thee?
Can I not weave thee nor fold thee
In with thy sisters to staying?
Vain is my passion or praying,
Rose from the rose-tree swaying.

Wayward sweet rose from the rose-tree swinging.
Can I not pass thee, forget thee?
Can I not see to regret thee?
In—'mid thy kindred's close ringing.
Out—to my heart she comes winging,
Rose from the rose-tree swinging.

Cruel red rose from the rose-tree swaying.
Ever to worship thee, throne thee.
Never to lose thee or own thee.
Thy beauty to keep me from straying,
Thy thorns for my passionate praying,
Rose from the rose-tree swaying.

ONE DAY IN DECEMBER

'Every dog has his day.'
Well, dear, do you remember.

How you and I found a golden day
In the midst of a bleak December?

You smiled at the chance of our meeting,
I blushed as I turned away,
While our little world stood by in amaze,
With hands upheld in dismay.

We loosed the chain of our little boat,
And each took an oar in hand.
You spoke no word, but you looked at me,
And we rowed for love's sweet land.

You said, 'All earth's beauties I see in your face.'
I said, 'All earth's music you're speaking.'
And the keel of our little craft grated the while
On the silvery strand of our seeking.

You looked at me and I smiled on you—
(O sweet! it was golden weather)—
Then we laughed as the boat glided back from the shore
And we pulled from the land together.

For you thought, perhaps, of another face,
And I—let pass, you remember,
Not half we said on that summer's day
We found in a bleak December.

IN WINTRY WEATHER

Dear, in wintry weather,
How close we crept together!
The storms, with all their thunder,
Could not our fond hands sunder.
No sorrow followed after,
Cold words or scornful laughter.
How close we crept together,
Through all the wintry weather!

Dear, when each rose uncurled
To its sweet narrow world,
You went to cull their glory;
You would not hear my story,
Too sweet the birds were singing,
Too fair the buds were swinging.

If I should come or go
You did not care to know.

When each sweet rose uncurled
To its unknown world,
How could you e'er remember
That in a bleak December,
Through all the bitter weather
We crept so close together?

MY ROSE

Droop all the flowers in my garden,
All their fair heads hang low;
For rose their fairest companion
Never again will they know.
Bring me no flowers for wearing,
Take these strange buds away.
For I cannot now have the fairest;
My rose that has died to-day.

What has blighted my blossom?
Stricken it down with death,
Over the walls of my garden.
What save the world's cold breath?
Then bring me no flowers for wearing,
Take these strange buds away.
Since I cannot now have the sweetest;
My rose that has died to-day.

THE AWAKENING

I had no culture for my love,
Hungrily my heart cried:
'Knowledge, be my master,
Turn, brain, O faster.
Grind the seeds of wisdom fine,
Till no mind be wise as mine,
At my wit in smiting
Men will smile delighting.
'Tis not too quick for craft, or
Not too keen for laughter.'
Wise for love's sweet sake to be
Surely is no vanity.

I had no fairness for my love.
Hungrily my heart cried:
'Beauty, be my handmaid!
Leave me unafraid,

That another glass had shown
Fair a face as hath my own.'
So the early morning
Found me still adorning,
Going from the glass with pride,
Coming back unsatisfied.
Vain for love's sweet sake to be
Surely is no vanity.

Lo! my love was not my love.
Stonily my heart cried:
'Take a fool for master,
Turn, brain, O faster,
While the jingling bells repeat
Much the chaff and little wheat.
Behind a pair of soul-lit eyes
You a soul would fain surprise.
None wise as he you ne'er could know,
Because a sweet tongue tells you so.
All his deeds were done before;
All his thoughts a borrowed store.
Said I, "He is heaven-sent
With his thinking brows so bent,"
This false light that made my day
Was the sun's reflected ray,
Dancing broken on the wave
Of ignorance, nor can I save

One tossing spark of foolish light
To make a beacon for my night.
Blind for love's sweet sake to be,
Seeing is a misery.'

A SUMMER'S DAY

Well, love, so be it as you say,
Just the hours of a summer's day,
And no sighing for what comes after,
Whether it is tears or laughter.

Take my hand, and we go together
Into love's land of golden weather.
You to be king and I for queen;
Right royally to reign, I ween.

Cool amber wine in cups of gold
Bring maids, in rosy fingers' hold,
Lip-pledged, but, you'll say ere your drinking,
My kiss were sweeter to your thinking.

And youths shall rob the spring for me
Of all the perfumed flowers that be;
I'll seek your eyes and they refusing,
I'll answer only at your choosing.

So, love, your hand, and we away,
Just the hours of a summer's day.
And no weeping for what comes after—
If it be tears, we've had our laughter.

PRE-EXISTENCE

We have met, you and I, long ago,
Yesterday when I saw you I knew,
For the sight of the city was gone.
And the sky took an eastern blue;
Strange flowers and strange perfumes were there,
Strange birds without song flitted by,
O I loved you as woman ne'er loved
When we met long ago, you and I.

We have loved long ago, you and I,
Though to-day we but linger to part.
O say, do you wish to forget ?
Does no answer awake in your heart?
Perhaps in the future 'tis writ
That we meet once again. Ah, good-bye!
You forget, but I sigh for that past
Where we met and we loved, you and I.

A MOTH

I, like a moth to the candle,
Am chained by a glance from your eye.

If I shun you, the world is in darkness;
If I seek my desire, I die.

I hide 'neath the wings of my fancy,
I seek out my room's darkest shade;
Your shining still follows me ever,
Till I fly to my doom unafraid.

And yet, in my seeking I shun you,
In shunning I seek for love's sake;
My wings will draw near you, not save me,
Like a bird's 'neath the eye of a snake.

Have pity; I watched from my shadow
A brother's wings fall 'neath your touch.
Loved you not the joy of his flitting?
Or is pride's cold victory such

That you laugh as he crawls from your glances,
Or dies in his pain at your feet,
So hopeless, untrusting, despairing,
Now hating the light that was sweet?

Have pity; a hand in its kindness
Once opened the casement to me,
'Go forth, foolish fly, for your life's sake.
Go forth ! in the night you are free.

'God's lamps in the Heavens are glowing,
More fair is their lighting than this
That was lit with a spark from man's fingers.
Go forth! lest you die in a kiss.'

The light of the stars could not reach me,
The warmth of your flame on my heart,
Too kind in their pity to wall me,
The fingers that saved were apart.

Have mercy, my life that my death is.
Blind, blind to your shining I fly.
If I shun you, the world is in darkness.
If I seek you, God help me! I die.

A MISUNDERSTANDING

I crave of you pardon to-day,

Yesterday I was mad when I spoke;
But the dream of our friendship was fair,
And my heart seemed to die when I woke.

I forgot when the fair image grew
Till a goddess's beauty it bore,
That the beautiful moulding was mine,
The clay was but clay as before.

I slept by a fountain one eve,
And thirsting awakened to drink;
But the waters I dreamt of were gone,
The young grass lay dead on the brink.

Did I think that the sun of to-day
Would shine out to-morrow as fair?
Did I vow this sweet breeze would return.
That now lifts with soft fingers my hair?

Then I were a fool so to dream:
So, friend, grant your pardon to me.
She I loved and I lost was not you,
But what I had wished you to be.

WHEN SUMMER COMES

When summer comes, then you are near to me,
I feel your phantom presence on my heart.
In every wind the dead year speaks again,
And every scene springs up to take its part.

Twas such a day, as sweet a wind arose.
To kiss with perfumed lips your blown hair;
With brow perplexed and that odd smile you had,
I wondered what you thought of, standing there.

Twas here, I stooped to pluck a drooping flower,
You prayed so foolishly that you might keep;
And here you turned a moment's space so cold,
I only laughed for fear that I should weep.

O phantom love! that haunts me restlessly.
That from my passionate hands will ever fly,
Fate owes me this, I will pursue and hold.
Or, finding you but shadow, let me die.

MONICA

Pardon give to Monica,
She is so very fair—
Though soft eyes give promises
Rosy lips forswear.
From the shy droop of her head,
You a hope might take;
In the hiding cheek, beware,
The dainty dimples wake.
Pardon give to Monica.

Pardon give to Monica,
The havoc of her eyes,
Yours they will not shun or seek,—
There the mischief lies.
If the flirting lashes thus
Make your day and night,
Would the loosing of your bonds
Give your heart respite?
Pardon give to Monica.

Pardon give to Monica,
She is so very fair.
What those cruel lips may say,
Roguish eyes forswear.
What knight's heart amid ye all
Were not glad to break.
That the lips with pity droop,
While eyes their laughter take?
Pardon give to Monica.

CLOUDS

Laughter and song for my cheer,
Life is so fair.
None so happy as I
Anywhere;
Birds in the woods carol clear,
White clouds in the sky.

Song silent and brow with a frown.
Why is this so?
Guiltless am I

Would you know,
The lark from the heavens drops down;
Gray clouds in the sky.

Sighing and tears for my sorrow,
Life is so drear.
None so weary as I,
'Tis a mere
Waste of love, and a wish for to-morrow—
Black night in the sky.

OUT WITH THE WORLD

I'm out with all the world to-day,
So all the world to me is gray,
Ah me! the bonny world.
Glad birds are building in the tree.
For them I have no sympathy;
From out the grove a thrush pipes clear,
I have no wish his song to hear;
From tangled boughs that young buds share
With last year's leaves, a startled hare
A moment peeps and then away;
I have no laughter for his play,
For all the sunny sky is gray.
The weariest I am to-day
In all the weary world.

Perchance to-morrow's hidden store
May bring my heart's content once more,
The sweet young spring comes very fair
With summer's breath and golden air;

And I may think there cannot be
A maid so blessed on land or sea.
Tm out, though, with the world to-day,
So all the world to me is gray,
Ah me! the bonny world.

THE SEEKING OF CONTENT

Sweet Content, at the rich man's gate,
Called, 'Wilt thou let me in?'
'No! thou art poor and thou art not great,

Hast nothing thy way to win.
Here love is little and mighty is power;
Fate may change in a wayward hour,
A monarch's heart may grow weary of thought.
What if his gold-bringing bees be caught,
Or wake to the fact of their sting?
He has all to lose, if nothing to gain,
And his throne doth lean for support in the main
On the different minds that have crowned him a kin
In their summer of thinking: so, sorrow
And winter may come with the morrow.'

Sweet Content, at the poor man's door.
Called, 'May I enter here?'
'No! we bees of the golden store
Are smothered with cold and fear.

We up with the sun to delve and moil,
We give our eyes with the midnight oil,
Till the sight burns dim, till the wick's no more,
To give our masters a coach-and-four,
To spatter us with the mire.
If nothing to lose, we have all to win.
To a heart's despair sin scarce seems sin—
When hope dies out, maybe crime steals in,
And patience may sometime grow sick and tire.
The wearied bee may die on the wing,
Or—God has given to each his sting.'

Sweet Content, at death's black gates,
Called, 'Wilt thou take me in?'
'Enter into the home of peace,
Close my gates on good and sin.
Shut on the poor man's rags my door.
Shut on the rich man's coach-and-four.
Nothing had man when life gave him breath.
Nothing he takes past the gates of death
Of the world's unequal paying.
Save only the joys he fought self to resign,
Only the sorrows he did not repine.
The sins that he stooped for, or passed, and Divine
Is the justice that judges the weighing.
What better reward for a tired life spent,
Than thee for his bride. Content?'

THE FATE OF THE THREE SONS OF UISNEACH AND DEIRDRÉ, DAUGHTER OF FEILIM

Woe to thee, daughter of Feilim! woe to thee, Deirdré,
Slain for thy sake were the three sons of Uisneach, and red
Grew the broad plains of Ulster, on Connaught unnumbered the dead.
Woe to thee, Deirdré!—Deirdré, daughter of Feilim.
Smiled the sweet babe in the face of the Druid and his warning.
Held her young mouth for his kissing, and wept at his scorning.
'King Connor, there's woe for thy pity, this woman-child born.
This bud of sweet promise will wound herself red with her thorn.
O King, in the future I prophesy evil before thee.
With the life of this child. Wilt thou listen and heed to my story?

The breath of a babe? or Connaught and Ulster in sorrow?
Let her be slain. Who remembers the deed on tomorrow?'
A dozen swords spring from their scabbards and flash fierce and bright,
The child for the fair steel stretched out her small hands in delight.
Connor laughed: 'Let her live, and if beauty should grant her a dower,
I will wed. Toast your queen, ere I hide her from fate in a tower.'

So the child prattled and grew fair as a wild-flower uncurled,
Till the maid's reason began to wonder how narrow her world.
What the great walls of the court hid from her inquisitive view,
What perfumed the wind from the west, and where went the finch when he flew.
Many sweet tales told her nurse, that fed her romantic young brain.
Till sleeping were sweet for its dreams, and waking was dreaming again.
What if their lone tower was built on a high rock right out in the sea.

Like the rock in that fountain of hers? or perhaps it might be
The world were a garden of flowers. Comes a prince in a boat—
That dream-prince of hers — (thrice a raven, with threatening note,
Flaps his wings) — or mayhap on an elf steed he'd ride.
High walls could not stay him. She leaned from her casement and cried:
'Look, nurse, they have slain a young deer in the courtyard below,
And the raven awaits them. My prince shall have skin like yon snow.
As red as that blood be his lip, and his hair like the raven's black wing.'
'Hush, dearest!' the woman replied. 'Hush, dearest, and think on the King.'
'O, nurse, were the pretty flower safe to live on the ocean's broad breast?
Would the little wren fly for her home and her mate to the eagle's cold nest?'
'Peace, childie! last night the wolf-hound howled long 'neath thy window-sill there.'
'Sweet nurse! dost thou know of a youth, so pure-skinned, with raven-dark hair?'

'Peace, child I know the death-watch ticked night long at thy own bed-head,
And a cock crew thrice out of hours.' 'Oh, nurse! and with lips blood-red?'
'Darling, in Connor's famed court, I've heard of as fair a young knight.'
'Oh, nurse! I've loved him in dreams. Wilt bring him but once to my sight?'
Woe to thee, fair child of sorrow. Love laughs at high walls in derision.

Woe to Naois and Ainlé and Ardan, who rescued thee safe from thy prison.

Into the mouth of the lion they flew from the lion pursuing,
For Scotia's king saw the bride's face—loved the beauty that was her undoing,
And many were slain for her sake, till the brave sons of Ulster have spoken:
'Lo, King! it were sad, for one maid, that our armies were scattered and broken.'
And Connor, aloud, to those chiefs, bade the three sons of Uisneach return—
Forgiven, come home to their land. But his heart was still hot with the burn
Of the shame of the maiden's desertion, and her scorn of a king and his glory;

He thought that the lips of the world must be glad on the theme of his story.
Tricked by a girl! how his pride turned the word, till Hate made it, in growing,
Fly back to the Druid and his warning. So this was the seed of his sowing.

He half thought it was writ on his brow, that the people were sick of their laughter;
He turned the stone in his sleeve: 'Let them laugh; he laughs best who laughs after.'
So Eogan, at word of the King, when he heard that the three youths had landed,
Was to welcome the brothers to Erinn, outspoken to seem and free-handed—
'But,' this in a whisper aside, 'slay them, each man, without warning.'
So by the sword of a traitor fell AinM, Ardan and Naois, for scorning
Of a king by the daughter of Feilim. And Deirdré was brought to King Connor.
What heeded she of his laughter, the sneers or the slights put upon her?
Since Naois was dead, her beloved, the rose on her cheek paled with sorrow.
And laughter was dead on her lips, only tears were her own night and morrow,

Till the King a new vengeance had planned to wake her strange listlessness to life:
To Eogan, the slayer of Naois, he gave the sad Deirdré to wife.
And Deirdre smiled once in his face as she mounted the steed by his side,
That was chafing to bear her away and bring the false Eogan his bride.
Never such quarry was seen as Connor's men hunted that day,
Never such laughter was heard as they followed up valley and brae,
For Connor the King for his vengeance was spending his courser's hot breath,
But Deirdré, the daughter of Feilim, was racing her brown steed for Death.

Woe to thee, daughter of Feilim! woe to thee, Deirdré!
Slain for thy sake were the fair sons of Uisneach, and red
Grew the broad plains of Ulster, on Connaught unnumbered the dead—
Woe to thee, Deirdré, Deirdré, daughter of Feilim!

THE BRIDAL OF LADY AIDEEN

O Lady Aideen, will you wed with me, wed with me in the early morning?
A silken gown for your body's wear, a golden crown for your hair's adorning.
(One flirting magpie on the quicken tree flies from his perching 'twixt you and me.)
The proudest colt that my land has fed
For you shall chafe first harnessed.
And for your bidding six maidens be.
(O bird of sorrow, 'tween hope and me!)

O Earl Desmond, I am loath to speak, loath to speak for your true heart's sorrow,
I'll be a bride at no man's altar, though I be a wedded bride to-morrow.
Death's hand closes on the digging spade ; rest for ever 'neath the yew-tree's shade.)

Six slow steeds will my body bear,
To fret or prance they will not care,
And no handmaiden with me would dwell
(Hark! the tolling of the passing bell.)

O Lady Aideen, will you name for me, name for me who won my refusing?
Who hath the singing and all the sun on earth for ever and I the losing?
(Oh, the plough horses going off from me, sorrow and tears will my harvest be.)
My arms were strong for your woman's fear;
My heart were weak for your loving, dear.
What can he give whom you will not name?
(Clings a winding-sheet by the candle's flame.)

O Earl Desmond, be you brave for sorrow, brave for sorrow which is no man's shielding;
Love has wept till his eyes grew blind, and victory's not in a weapon's yielding.
(Six black horses awaiting me, the ring of the spade has ceased to be.)
My lord is named with a bated breath.
Whom hope calls 'Life' and despair names 'Death.'
And, oh, his love no world can kill!
(The banshee waits on the window-sill.)

LADY KATHLEEN

Fair Lady Kathleen in her tower
Bowed her head like a wounded flower;
Wept she the weary night away;
'Here I spin for a year and a day,
But 'tis for love's sweet sake,' she said,
'My heart must break and I were dead.
The nettle I've pulled when the moon was bright
And brought it home in the dark of night —
I've trod it soft 'neath my naked feet
To make a cloak for thy rescue, Sweet!'
The Lady Kathleen wept full sore:
'Oh, misery mine for a year and more!'

Day after day, and a promised spring
Bloomed into a summer of blossoming.
A thrush was carolling, mad with glee.
On the topmost bough of the elm-tree;

He sang to fair Kathleen in her tower,
But the maiden heeded nor bird nor flower.

The daisies white and the sweet wild rose
Clad mead and hedge in their summer snows.
Fair Lady Kathleen wept alway:
'Oh, misery mine for a year and a day!'

A ghostly moon in a steel cold sky,
A dance of leaves by the wind swept by,
Like the mirthless rushing of phantom feet.
But the Lady Kathleen murmured: 'Sweet!
Love keeps a woman's summer young.'
She sped without fear in the awe of night,
Though the shuddering shadows would stay her flight
With the thought of a horror unknown,
Or a streamlet would laugh 'neath the hedge unshown;
But Lady Kathleen wept no more:
'Oh, joy is mine, for my trial's o'er!'

To the white thorn-tree on the fairy rath
The Lady Kathleen quick took her path,
Till she stood in the midst of the elfin host.
Like a lily pale or a fair white ghost.
Loud the fairies laughed in their mad retreat.
As she found her love with a whispered 'Sweet!
It were no sorrow to lose for you
Youth's golden days or weep long nights through.'

But he said: 'My love she had golden hair —
Her hands, her feet, they were lily-fair:
So *you* can never be love of mine.'

'O Love!' she cried, 'if I am not thine,
My hands grew hard as they wove for thee
The magic cloak that hath set thee free.
My face grew sad, and my hair grew white,
In the silent horror of many a night.
And what shall I now that hope's beacon-glow
Is quenched, and my heart sinks with gloom and woe?
Thy love,' she cried, 'be she lily- fair
As the fruit-tree's bloom that may never bear,
Thou hungeredst — to fruit the blossom came:
Thus youth was lost and thus beauty slain.
Thy Sweet was fair as the page unwrit
Till Love's strong hand traced his name on it.
Then, O my dear, if thou canst not see
This sorrow cometh from love of thee,

Be blind awhile with a rising tear.
And thou wilt find that thy love is here.'
But ah for woman whose heart is strong
To weary never and love too long!
And what is life to a heart denied?
Fair Lady Kathleen drooped and died.

THE FLIGHT OF THE WILD GEESE

Wrapt in the darkness of the night,
Gathering in silence on the shore,
Wild geese flown from hiding on the hills
(Hark! the wolf-hound; thrice he howled before),
Wild geese with forest leaves tangled in their hair.
Is that blood on the heaving breasts of some.
Or dull red clay from fox-deserted lair?
Why thus so stealthy do they come?
Wild geese, women's arms round you in the darkness;
Women's hearts forbid to cry though they break;
Little children must not sob in their kissing;
'Brother, forever? O hush thee, for God's sake!'
Wild geese with fierce eyes, deathless hope in your hearts.
Stretching your strong white wings eager for your flight.
These women's eyes will watch your swift returning.
(Thrice the banshee cried in the stormy night.)

Flinging the salt from their wings, and despair from their hearts,
They arise on the breast of the storm with a cry and are gone.
When will you come home, wild geese, with your thousand strong?
(The wolf-dog loud in the silence of night howls on.)
Not the fierce wind can stay your return or tumultuous sea,
Nor the freedom France gives to your feet on her luxuriant shore.
No smiles for your love like the tears of your sorrowing land.
Only Death in his reaping could make you return no more.
White birds, white birds, I dream of that glad homecoming;
Though human eyes could not mark your silent flight,
Women lie face down with clenched hands in the sea.
(Thrice the banshee cries in the stormy night.)

A SINGING BIRD IN THE CITY

Golden-throated, hath God sent thee for our comfort in the city?
Sweet, sweet! singing, singing all the day.
I said: Ah, the young Spring she will lure him from his pity,

And he'll seek the sunny distance in the May.

For all the other birds have left us lonely
That sought us when the hungry winter came;
Quick they forgot, and he remembered only,
But with the breath of Spring he'll fly the same.

For the daffodil is nodding, just awaking,
With a sunny ray imprisoned in its breast;
Over purple violets the hawthorn buds are breaking —
There a perfect Eden for a nest.

There, I said, the lazy cattle in the sunshine will be resting,
Dreaming in the pasture lands where summer airs blow sweet,
Or standing in the river to feel each slow wave cresting
In snowy pearl bracelets around their cloven feet.

But here they gasp and stumble, foot-sore and full of sorrow;
No question 'Why these sufferings?' to the careless passer-by
In thtir patient weary eyes that shall see no fair tomorrow,
And find no balm of tears as they stagger on to die.

I said: A feathered choir in the leafy heights are singing
A farewell to the West where the evening sun dreams low,
And the passion of their song sets their budding perch slow swinging,
Till the moon with silver sail glides through the afterglow.

Here, crimeless prisoners caged, they sigh and dream for ever
Of a lonely mate in some cool grove that droops beside her brood;
They beat the cruel bars in a passionate endeavour
To hush the little voices that call in vain for food.

They dream of autumn colours, the crimson of the cherries,
The breath of heaven's glory o'er the fields of yellow corn;
They sigh for draughts delicious from juicy rowan berries,
The breath of heaven in the air, so fresh and fair the morn.

How they rested on the wind or pierced the low clouds flying
Across the storm-swept heaven, that barred and distant sky!
Men gave a plot of grass—all earth's wide range denying—
Scarce large enough to sod them when they die.

I said: Of sight of kingcups and cowslips yellow gleaming,
No avaricious eye will envious loose its hold,
Nor will a greedy hand, where the celandine lies dreaming,
Dart hungrily to rob her of her gold.

There is an end of passion—a joy reigns there for ever,

That the storm's great exultation cannot conquer or displace;
Here is an end of quiet, and weary hearts rest never.
Lest coming feet should crush them in the passion of life's race.

There amidst long fern and perfumed breath of heather
A laughing river wakes far up the mountain-side,
To meet a hundred streams and join their songs together
As they glance through mead and woodland to meet the restless tide.

But here the mourning river flows past in sullen sorrow —
In her shamed desecration she hurries to the sea;
She hath heard full many cries that sought a great tomorrow,
Many a desperate soul that curst the laws that be.

Many griefs are covered by her dark mantle flowing,
Many a cold white face lies hidden on her breast;
With her, men would escape the reaping of their sowing,
Sad women give their souls for her sweet rest.

I said: When he has heard how hollow is our laughing,
Seen Crime and gray Despair creep hand in hand with Night,
How Failure spills the cup Ambition fills for quaffing,
How Love is timid, coming to Care's sight.

I said in discontentment: 'Oh, who hath heart for singing?
Go seek some worthier spot for thy sweet lay.'
But through the changing summer until bare boughs are swinging,
He goes singing, singing, singing all the day.

A CRY IN THE WORLD

Kine, kine, in the meadows, why do you low so piteously?
High is the grass to your knees and wet with the dew of the morn,
Sweet with the perfume of honey, and breath of the clover blossoms;
But the sad-eyed kine on the hillside see no joy in the day newborn.
'Man, man has bereft us and taken our young ones from us;
Thus we call in the eve, call through night to the break of day,
That they may hear and answer; so we find no peace in the meadows.
Our hearts are sad with hunger for the love man stole away.'

Bird, bird, on the tree-top, my heart doth sigh for thy music;
In the glad air of morn and promise of summer, rejoice!

Thy head droops low on thy breast, half hid in thy ruffled feathers,
The grove is lone for thy singing, O bird of the silver voice!
'Man, man has bereft me, stolen my nestlings from me,

Wrecked the soft home we built 'mid the budding blossoms of spring.
My mate's brown wings grow red in vain beating the bars of her prison;
With heart so full of longing and mourning, how can I sing?'

Seal, in the cliff's shadow, why are thine eyes so mournful?
Come from the gloom and the echo of the sea's sighs in the cave,
Sink down into deeper waters 'mid the hidden flowers of the ocean,
Or seek the splash and sparkle 'neath the snowy break of the wave.
'Man, man has bereft me, robbed me of those my loved ones;
Alone, I find no gladness; alone, where is joy for me
In the silvery flash of the fish or the wonderful gardens of coral?
My eyes grow dim with watching the desolate waste of the sea!'

Woman, king of the world is the babe you hush with sobbing,
King of all that is living in air or sea, or on land.
Therefore why do you kiss with lips that are dumb with sorrow?
Your tear-drops falling cold have chilled the little hand.
This is the soul's proud right, the earth given into his keeping;
And all that lives thereon must come to his feet a slave.
Mother, why do you flee with haggard eyes in the morning?
To answer with white face hid in the grass of a baby's grave.

I WOULD HAVE WEPT

I would have wept with the beast,
The bird, the blossoming flower,
The hundred years of the oak.
Or the insect born for an hour,

Saying with my soul's right:
Ah, woe for your body's pain!
Therein you must die, and pass
Into dust, without hope of gain.

From the weary feet's toiling to spring
To oblivion, and never to know
That the horrible pains of the flesh
You have left in the body below;

That He leaves you an heirdom of pain.
And forgets you when dropped from His hand
That had mercy for us; you would die
In your grief, could you understand.

But the oxen looked up as I spoke,
For a moment in mild surprise,

Then bent again to the yoke,
With peace in their dreaming eyes.

And a small brown bird on her nest
Hid her speckled eggs with care,
Lest one should chill while her mate
Sang high in the golden air.

Still the flower and tree 'neath the sun
Unfolded their buds to bloom;
And the fly, clad in sombre gray,
Danced over the faint perfume.

And the sun coming forth from a cloud
Shone fair on a smiling land.
I said: Hush, questioning heart;
'Tis *you* cannot understand.

WHAT WE MUST DO

What we must do and may not do.
This is the World's whole refrain,
Till beating on the wearied brain,
We wonder what is true.

My love! my love! who passes by,
As Fate hath willed ere we were born,
Could I but face the people's scorn.
And tell my love, or die.

But this is not a woman's part,
A careless brow you dare to show;
She smiles upon you as you go,
To hide a breaking heart.

My friend did take my hand to-day,
Light kisses laid upon my face;
My sad reproach was in its place—
She could not tell me Nay!

How poor we are with all our laws
Of ever-changing form and dress!
The world becomes a weariness,
Life's current choked with straws.

I sometimes think the brain more wise

Where madness reason hath out-thrown,
And gave the fool a life his own,
That had no guilt in lies—

Than we, who claim to Reason's rule
And chain our freedom ruthlessly.
Not to what is, but what must be—
Forever in a school.

The ox, the ass, 'neath Nature's dome,
Follow His teachings without strife;
And yet they reach the heights of life.
And bring their harvest home.

I ask, O World, a wider sight
For men, that they to see be strong—
Your little wrongs that are not wrong,
Your little rights that are not right.

There's not so much sin here below
As petty fashions make believe;
Yet so the world's sad eyes deceive—
Sin is much greater than they know.

A STORM

Come, teasing wind, we will fly,
Seek our heart's desire, you and I;
Fit comrade for me,
Thou breath of liberty,
I sigh for the freedom of your wings.
The sea will make us horses for our speed.
The fields will give the perfume of their seed,
In the woods a sweet rose blowing
We will scatter it in going.
And bear the lark up sunward as he sings.

Go! we must part, you and I;
Not *this* my heart's desire, so good-bye!
Had I thought a moment's madness
Had wrought so dire a sadness.
My soul had never sorrowed for thy wings.
What have the tossing waves found for their play?
Have mercy, let the white face hide away!

In the fields a harvest dead,
In the woods life's promise fled,
And the lark is blown seaward as he sings.

Far better you were sleeping, O my soul.
Than that your coming forth a moment stole
From another's heart its rest.
Die you silent in my breast
And seek in death that answer life denied:
Lest a dying voice should curse instead of pray,
Lest a heart should shadow, blighted of its May,
Lest a soul glad of its light
Should be plunged in gloom of night.
Be in the World's seeing satisfied.

BUT FOR THE TEARS

'The World were a place to play in,' said the children
'The play-ground of the present; all that is have we,
No past is ours to sorrow,
No clouding thought of morrow,
And joy is slow in passing where we be.
With knowledge of a soul's right scarce awake.
Life had no fears:
The World were good to play in,' said the children,
'But for the tears.'

'The World were good to love in,' said the youth.
'With a future all our own to dream and do,
With a fate for our soul's making,
Fame for our manhood's taking,
And Hope will never shun as we pursue.
Crowned with knowledge of a soul our calm and fair horizon clears;
And the World were good to love in,' said the youth,
'But for the tears.'

'The World were good to die in,' said the aged,
'When lost years come to haunt you with their groans.
When dead dreams won't be stilled,
And hopes long unfulfilled
Beat on your bleeding heart nor heed its moans,
With knowledge of a soul's right gained and lost,
Less love endears
Some little your poor flesh, O welcome, death, to age.
Save for those tears.'

A RECOMPENSE

I raised my hands against my fate,
I struck her frowning brows between;
'I will be good, I will be great,
No matter what has been.

'What care I if before my time
Dead men their passions left to me?
Can I not tune my life to rhyme
From discord played by thee?'

She struck my pencil from my grasp,
And here my first ambition ends.
How bitterly the loss unmans!
She had so many friends.

Love saw my struggle and was glad;
For love's sweet sake I struggled on,
Till love grew tired loving, then
I cursed the sun that shone.

'I'll strive no more against my fate,'
I said, 'I will give up, go down—'
But friendship caught my idle hands
And would not let me drown.

For friendship's sake I tried once more,
Till love stole friendship from my side;
I cursed the friend that gained the boon
That was to me denied.

The hound that followed at my heel
Looked up with eyes so full of love
kissed the curly brows between
And blessed the God above.

ECLIPSE

So for the luxury of the flesh, wrap it in fur of fox that it be warm,
In the bear's coat sheltering its nakedness from storm.
Give wine for its hot veins, fame for its throne, and laughter for its lips,
All ends in one eclipse,
Sunshine or snows.

We gain a grave, and afterwards—God knows.

Bemoan beside your fire your own particular fate, that evil wind
That blows for you no mercy, think till the wearied mind
Doth ease itself in tears, or reason from her high throne slips,
So ends life in eclipse
However the wind blows.
We gain a grave, and afterwards—God knows.

'And wherefore is all this?' you question me, 'this weighing of rich and poor,
Of many tears and laughter of which no mind hath cure?'
Nought save 'twere thinking for a winter's night, till my mind trips
O'er thought and finds eclipse
For smiles and woes,
And I a grave, and afterwards—God knows.

REMORSE

'Where have you been, my pale, pale son, all night in the winter storm?'
(Hark! the joy-bells chime in their passionate rhyme.)
'O mother! the bird is sheltered, the beast housed warm—
And they, with their bodies' comfort, are thus content;
But I, in debt for a soul, have the long night spent
In shunning the question of God, till the spirit within
Fought mad through the human walls of my quivering skin
At its kindred passion without in the howling night
'Where is thy brother?' O question not giving respite.
O mother! what do they answer, those lips, blood red,
Of nature, in sport with her thousand deaths? I questioned.
'Send me an answer.' She spoke not, the Mother of Death

Life rocked in her restless arms, while she sucked at her breath—
("Where?" the bells cry, and I dare not reply.)'

'What would you tell me, my child, my child, that once slept a babe on my breast?'
(Do the death-bells toll for a passing soul?)
'O mother! my friend is dead, now I stand confessed.
I can strike the stone into flame, make the dark give light,
But I cannot give back to the tiniest bird its flight.
I can easily shut life's gates, but God alone holds the key;
And all the darkness of night cannot shelter me.
For my friend, you understand, my friend is dead,
So people will pity the tears that my hot eyes shed.
No voice to cry "Guilty," not seeing my brain's red shame—
Not knowing that "Dead," in my heart, hath another name.
He wondered the world should plot him such mischief and pain;

Knew not that his world was worked from one jealous man's brain.
Whose hands set in motion the wheels, laid his heart on the rack,
Followed ever with murmurs of doubt on his fortunate track,

Till the world, more eager to listen to evil than good,
Caught my whispers to hurl them back on the man as he stood.
Crept scandal, with listening ears, to his keyhole, supplied
Quick rumour, with news for the keen appetites so denied;
And hungry excitement kept hard on his quicksilver feet
Till men, self-comparing, and finding comparing were sweet.
Would say, "Look at this man,"—meaning, look what a contrast there be,—
Or, "So has he sinned, see to him (so your gaze avoid me)."
Foolish world, as if men were not judged, by each different mind.
By God's justice, not that of the world's great classing of kind:
"This is right, that is wrong," as though minds were all made on one plan.
Leaving nought to inheritance, will-power, or surroundings of man.
He is dead, mother, dead; I his friend might have made his earth fair.
But I crept like a scorpion to sting all his hopes to despair:

Robbed his body of this world's joys, and his soul of the hope
Of that other that sings through the air at the pull of the rope,
Till my mad passion swells at the tongues of the bells.'

'Hush thee and listen, my son, my son, for the bells are the voice of love.'
(All the things He made live, can their Father forgive.)
'O mother! a sinner's cry may be heard above.
And so, if the dead forgive, then my dying breath
Will plead that a sad soul pass through the gates of death.
Where it stood outside so weary, afraid to call.
For that pale ghost standing within in his funeral pall,
Awaiting my tears that would wash his stained record white.
And I could not weep; but, mother, I weep to-night.'
(Peace, the bells sing, is God's reckoning.)

AVE MARIA

In the darkness of the night I awake and weep,
Ave Maria, hear my cry!
Dread shapes crowd around me, I cannot sleep,
Ave Maria, hear my cry!

Love that must separate, Death that takes all,
(Ave Maria, hear my cry!)
Comes in the darkness with shuddering footfall,
Ave Maria, hear my cry!

Stern seems the face of the Lord and turned away,
(Ave Maria, hear my cry!)
For my prayerless night and my deedless day,
Ave Maria, hear my cry!

Thou art meek and full of mercy, pray for me,
Ave Maria, hear my cry!
He will listen to my prayer for love of thee,
Ave Maria, hear my cry!

Say that the world's dust was in my eyes,
Ave Maria, hear my prayer!
Say that my ears were deaf with city cries,
Ave Maria, hear my prayer!

Say that man and beast so questioned,
(Ave Maria, hear my cry!)
That on the cross He hung beloved but dead.
Ave Maria, hear my cry!

In the darkness of the night I awake and weep,
Ave Maria, hear my cry!
All that I am not wakes my soul from sleep,
Ave Maria, hear my cry!

ONE WHO IS DEAD

Never again, my darling, never again,
Till the gates of God are open for me to pass,
May we join our parted hands that loosed their hold,
Ere Death's cold fingers closed on thine. Alas!
Feeling palm from palm was slipping in finger's hold,
Had you but spoken or I shed a tear.
This had not been, but now you have forgot,
And I remember only I held you dear.

THE END OF THE WORLD

Even the silent lips and comforting calm face
I had no more; I took my place
Still wondering, behind the slow sad coach that bore
All of your beauty Death could rob from me,
One amongst many men who followed thee.

'Now comes an end of things,' I said, and faced the light
And saw the sun; there was not any night
Although the sands of your sweet life had run.
Even the little children, in their glee.
Raced by the four slow steeds that carried thee.

The curious passer's gaze I watched with jealous eyes
Your coffin find, through its disguise
Of living flowers, hid from their careless pity safe behind
Those wooden walls; oh, safe, my dear, no one shall see.
Or none remember save those who follow thee.

Even the little birds and blossoming spring flowers,
They did not care, and still the hours
Went on to weave slow days to years for me to bear.
No song was hushed, no laughter stilled for me,
No woman wept when my world died with thee.

SEEKING

There I cannot find thee, O my love!
In the city's clamour,
In its pleasure's glamour;
'Mid the multitude of faces
Or the wilderness of places,
There I cannot find thee, O my love!

There I cannot find thee, O my love!
Where corn groweth yellow,
Where luscious fruits come mellow.
Where 'neath the roses swinging
Hide birds that wake to singing.
There I cannot find thee, O my love!

There I cannot find thee, O my love!
Where sweeps the snowy pinion
O'er the seamew's wide dominion;
Where the gull unceasingly
Screams a chorus to the sea,
There I cannot find thee, O my love!

There I cannot find thee, O my love!
Blind in the dark my seeking,
I stand with lone heart breaking,
With hushed and listening breath
I gaze through the gates of death—

There I cannot seek thee, O my love!

WEARY

Here, in the silent churchyard, 'mid a thousand dead, alone.
Weary I sit for a moment clasping this cross of stone,
Weary of worldly passions of selfishness, greed, and sin.
Grant me the shade of thy wings, O Death, for I would rest within.
Weary of smiling faces when the heart is like to break.
Of lips that are too silent when they long the while to speak,
Of tears that fall from eyes too young, of quivering lips that laugh.
Of the ceaseless clatter of tongues, who plead in none save their own behalf.

O desolate grave beside me, by pity and love forgot,
The calm eyes of peace watch o'er you — I hunger for such a spot;
The tender sprays of ivy, that clung to your cross alone,
Have died in the spring of their living, and turned like it to stone;

So trusting, believing, and loving, these foolish dreams of a child,
I dreamt of the joy of living in a world so undefiled.
Ah! blighted my hope's young promise by that same cold world's breath.
I am weary; grant me the shade of thy wings, that I may rest, O Death!

Weave wreaths of Truth's fair blossoms for my home when my lips are mute.
I gathered its rosy apples and found them hut Dead Sea fruit,
And take from the world's garden my flowers that Hope planted there,
That, turning to weeds in their growing, were culled by the hand of Despair.
Weary of worldly sorrows, of longings unfilled and regret,
Grant me the shade of your wings, O Peace! that I may sleep and forget.

GRAY EYES

Sitting alone in my room,
Alone in the gathering gloom,
Solitude in the rest of the tomb.
While the drip, drip, drip of the rain,
Like tears that are falling in vain
For a loss that is gone past regain,
Falls soft on the window-pane
Of my room.

Alone, alone, alone.
And no one to hear my moan
In the world's great heart of stone;

Only poverty that wakes disgust,
Only promises light as dust,
And nought that is true or just,
Cold hearts that you cannot trust —
Alone.

Weary of hopes that fade.
Of a life that is one long shade

Of joys that bloom decayed,
Fall cool on my heart, O rain,
Till you soften this bitter pain,
This ice that doth it enchain —
Oh, let it once hope again,
Or fade.

Ye who in the crowd pass by,
Not giving a glance or a sigh,
Not heeding my lonely cry.
Oh, pause, and say, ere you go,
Is there love in that world you know?
You have caused me all my woe.
Gray eyes, gray eyes, ah! so
Pass by.

IN SOUTHERN SEAS

In southern seas we sailed, my love and I,
In southern seas.
Death joined no chorus as the waves swept by,
No storm hid in the breeze.
Low keeled our boat until her white wings dipped half wet with spray,
And seeking gulls tossed on the passing wave laughed on our way.
The rhyme of sound, the harmony of souls—of silence, too;
Your silence held my thoughts, my love, as mine of you;
The winged whispering wind that blew our sails was summer sweet—
I found my long-sought paradise crouched at thy feet.

In northern seas I weep alone, alone,
In winter seas.
Death's hounds are on the waves, with many moans
Death's voice comes with the breeze;

My helpless boat, rocked in the wind, obeys no steadfast hand.
Her swinging helm and lashing sheet have lost my weak command;
The shrieking sea-birds seek the sheltering shore,

The writing waves leap upward, and their hoar
Strong hands tear at the timbers of my shuddering craft.
I cry in vain, the Fates have seen and laughed.
Time and the world have stormed my summer sea—
I ate my fruit, the serpent held the tree.

THE LEPER'S BETROTHED

To clasp his spirit undefiled, my spirit leaped beneath my hand,
He said no sad reproach to me, but only, 'Love, I understand.'
O coward my eyes that would not see, held slaves 'neath closing finger-tips;
O coward my flesh that would not let my spirit's whisper through your lips.

He might have said, 'This rose I pulled fell not to pieces at my touch;
The robin fled not at my gaze, nor hid from me her feathered clutch;
The evening moon arose as fair with my sad face to look upon;
The sun withdrew no single ray, caressed me as it shone;

The hound still follows at my heel, nor finds me less beloved for this—
But, oh! my love shrinks from my side and trembles at my kiss.
Would you find horror at my touch, or poison at my body's breath.
If but my flesh grew fair again, and my soul darkened with its death?'

God struck him with a fell disease, he said no sad reproach to me,
He left the world of men behind for that sad isle beyond the sea;
He loved the beautiful, the sun—and God has robbed him of that right,
Housed him with men that are not men, with horrors for his sight
And I, my love! have robbed from you the right of love, and hope, and trust.
And gave a woman's feeble dreams that God has razed to dust.
Oh, pity me, for I am weak, not worth that precious love you gave,
I weep undoing, while your ship finds you an island and a grave;

I curse my flesh that holds me down, my hidden face, my cowardly hand;
bless the parting voice that said, 'My love, I understand.

LAST EVE

Last eve as I leaned from my lattice, looked out at the night
Where the gray of the sea misted into the gray of the skies,
Came with quick beating of wings and long sorrowful cries
Beautiful birds, and I wept, being blind with their white.

How the wind's strong invisible hands beat on doorway and pane,
And the sea seemed to writhe and roar in an anguish of thought!

How the moon's frightened face looking down seemed to shun what she sought.
Hid so pale in cloud fingers to weep in a passion of rain!

They had come in the night, and the storm, winging back to my breast
These hopes that were hopeless, these dreams that were ever as dreams;
Rending my heart with sharp beaks and their passionate screams,
Leashing my soul with the storm from its haven of rest.

Night long did I put them away, did they turn again,
Till the tumultuous waves bore them out in their creepy recess,
Tossed them back on the reef with a deadly pretence of caress;
Flung up by the hand of the sea, beaten back by the lash of the rain.

White birds, it is over and done, your last passion has paled;
The world has no place for your flight nor my heart for your screams.
O hopes that were hopeless, sweet dreams that were ever as dreams,
Let go! get back to your graves, you have fought and have failed.

CEAN DUV DEELISH

Cean duv deelish, beside the sea
I stand and stretch my hands to thee
Across the world.
The riderless horses race to shore
With thundering hoofs and shuddering, hoar,
Blown manes uncurled.

Cean duv deelish, I cry to thee
Beyond the world, beneath the sea,
Thou being dead.
Where hast thou hidden from the beat
Of crushing hoofs and tearing feet
Thy dear black head?

Cean duv deelish, 'tis hard to pray
With breaking heart from day to day,
And no reply;
When the passionate challenge of sky is cast
In the teeth of the sea and an angry blast
Goes by.

God bless the woman, whoever she be,
From the tossing waves will recover thee
And lashing wind.
Who will take thee out of the wind and storm,
Dry thy wet face on her bosom warm

And lips so kind?

I not to know. It is hard to pray.
But I shall for this woman from day to day,
'Comfort my dead,
The sport of the winds and the play of the sea.'
I loved thee too well for this thing to be,
O dear black head!

GOOD-BYE!

And so good-bye, my love, my dear, and so good-bye,
E'en thus from my sad heart go hence, depart;
I cast thee out, renounce, and hold no more;
I wreck the cup of joy thou heldest for drinking
To my lips, thinking we'd quaff—be as before;
Yet at my laughter if thou hearest sigh.
And ask no question 'Why?'
Believing only that my pleasure lies
To find approval in thy pleased eyes.

Before our time, my dear, my dear. Fate so had planned
Our little race to run beneath the sun,
That we should meet and love and dream, then separate.
Perchance, she thought, though, there would be no parting,
No salt tears smarting; she deemed to mate
My most imperfect self to thine, and gain
A better harvesting of pain:

I weep, but null is Fate's decree—
Such tears fall not so bitterly.

I saw a woman once undo and then peruse
Old letters with hard eyes; through such disguise
I pierced and knew her weeping.
'And such he was,' she said. 'Whose is the failing
That love is paling? which is the soul that's sleeping?'
His step; and quick the letters put in hiding:
They meet with cold eyes chiding.
If I were such as she,
Oh, death were well for me!

I saw a man's gray eyes fill up, and overfull
Let fall two sparkling tears, as one who fears;
Draw forth a curling braid of woman's hair,
Lay it across his lips with swift caressing.

His love confessing: 'My sweet beyond compare,
Whose fault we love to-day and hate to-morrow?'
Her voice: he hides his sorrow,
And meets her bitterly;
And oh, if thou wert he!

I saw two children wondering, hand in hand.
Sit dumb beside their hearth, as if their mirth
Were stricken by some fear past understanding;
Find in their parents' eyes with silent reading
The old degrading truth beyond commanding—

The bond of love that held two hates united,
They plead still unrequited,
They grow and bear the thorn —
Oh, better never born!

Better if thou wert dead, my dear, if thou wert dead;
No woman's moan but mine should hush thy sleeping.
When other eyes should close, their watch forgetting,
Mine vain regretting still its watch was keeping;
When other hearts grew weary by death's gates.
Stole to their loves and hates.
Mine still lived for its laughter
In what might come hereafter.

Good-bye! I would not have thee dead. We grasped at stars
That only God could take: we tried to make
A paradise for keeping
Upon an earth where He had wrecked the garden;
Giving no pardon, baptized us all in weeping.
So pass; good-bye! Some other woman's love.
Oh! not as great as mine, will find above
Some happier fate to choose you
Than mine that did refuse you.

Dora Sigerson Shorter – A Concise Bibliography

Poetry Collections
Verses (1893)
The Fairy Changeling and Other Poems (1897)
The Collected Poems of Dora Sigerson Shorter (1907)
New Poems (1913)
The Sad Years (1918)
The Tricolour, Poems of the Irish Revolution (1922)

Novels
The Country-House Party (1905)
The Story and Song of Black Roderick (1906)
Through Wintry Terrors (1907)

Short Story collections
The Father Confessor, Stories of Death and Danger (1900)